Henry Herbert Godfrey

**A Souvenir of Musical Toronto**

Henry Herbert Godfrey

**A Souvenir of Musical Toronto**

ISBN/EAN: 9783337088866

Printed in Europe, USA, Canada, Australia, Japan

Cover: Foto ©Thomas Meinert / pixelio.de

More available books at **www.hansebooks.com**

## SECOND ANNUAL ISSUE,
### 1898-1899.

*" O Music! sphere-descended maid, Friend of pleasure, wisdom's aid!"* COLLINS.
*" Lighter move the minutes fledged with music."* TENNYSON.

# Musical Toronto

*" The harmony of things, as well as sounds, from discord springs."*
—SIR J. DENHAM.

*" Above all, music ought to be,—like poetry, and like all that is true, genuine, and grand,— simple and unaffected; it ought to be the exact, true, and natural expression of feeling."* —GLUCK.

### COMPILED BY H. H. GODFREY.

Entered according to the Act of Parliament of Canada in the year 1898, by H. H. Godfrey, in the office of the Minister of Agriculture.

BEETHOVEN.

SECOND EDITION,
1898-1899.

A.....

# Souvenir

OF.....

# Musical

# Toronto

" ' ' ' Music must achieve
Somewhere, some day, somehow,
All that is silent now;
And make articulate
The truths we could not speak,
The Love that pined away,
When Music claims her own,
O then, and then alone,
We shall ourselves for our past selves atone."

—From "An Ode to Music," by SERRANUS.

# SALUTATORY.

"Music exalts each joy." —*Armstrong*.

THE publication of the first edition of "Musical Toronto" (in the early part of 1897) was entered into with a certain amount of diffidence. It was a new departure, and there was no certainty as to how it would be received, either by the profession or the public.

So gratifying was its reception, however, that it was decided to repeat it with additions and corrections from time to time. It forms a reference book of a decidedly unique character for those who desire to engage musical talent of any description. It also forms a very interesting table book for the drawing-room or library, and is so used in thousands of homes from Halifax to Vancouver.

A few words from the editor may not be amiss as to the object, scope and arrangement of this little book.

The object is two-fold. First, it is intended as a compliment to the members of the musical profession. There is very little that is beautiful in the every-day life of the present age, but *to* that "little" music and musicians contribute far more than their share. Again, it was felt that the thousands of musicians or musical people scattered over the Dominion, who had received their musical education here, would hail with pleasure a souvenir of this character, which would present at a glance portraits of the artists under whom they had studied, and pictures of buildings and institutions rendered dear to them through long and affectionate association. The demand for copies has proved that he was right in this assumption.

UNIVERSITY COLLEGE, TORONTO.

The scope of the book is simply that of description—not criticism. As to the arrangement of its contents, the editor must frankly confess that his principal difficulty consisted in so laying them out as to avoid any appearance of giving precedence or instituting comparison.

The following order was finally decided upon:

The first article is general and—so far as possible—arranged in strictly *chronological* order. The second article treats of the study of music in the great Ladies' schools. The balance of the book is arranged in strictly *alphabetical* order.

This at least is the order which the editor has *endeavored* to follow, and if any errors or omissions have inadvertently occurred, he must crave the

VICTORIA COLLEGE, TORONTO.

kind indulgence of his readers on the plea of "good intentions." It must also be borne in mind that, small as the book may appear, it has required a very large amount of careful labor to collect and arrange the data necessary to write over a hundred separate biographical sketches, no matter how brief each sketch might be.

With these few words of explanation, we will proceed with our subject.

# The Art Divine.

FROM the earliest ages the highest test of civilization has been the cultivation of the Arts. A country may be prosperous in a material sense or softening literature, to enjoy a it may be successful in arms, but without the influence of the gentler arts of music, and painting, it cannot be truly considered high degree of civilization.

Of all the Arts, music the Art Divine probably exercises the greatest influence upon the minds of men. A rugged, simple peasantry cannot enjoy the beauties of painting, literature or sculpture it takes years of training and involves a certain amount of leisure to appreciate and enjoy these but music appeals instantaneously to the humblest and most unsophisticated. In its simpler forms it reaches the heart at once.

ST. JAMES' CATHEDRAL, TORONTO.

Even among the rudest and most martial races it acts as a spur and inspiration to further deeds of valor.

The singing of simple patriotic airs has had a wonderful cementing and unifying influence upon nations in times of doubt, disturbance and dissension, as witness the effect upon the French nation of the Marseillaise, upon the Germans of "The Watch on the Rhine" and upon the Italians of Garibaldi's Hymn. The English are not an emotional people, but no one can doubt that the singing of Rule Britannia has had more effect in impressing the fact of England's naval supremacy upon the masses than all the speeches ever spoken or all the statistics ever published.

TRINITY UNIVERSITY, TORONTO.

We in Canada were accused until recently and perhaps with reason of lacking in national spirit. We were English, French, Scotch or Irish but we were not Canadian, and a union with the nation to the south was considered as not improbable. But suddenly a new and different feeling sprang up as if by magic. We suddenly felt that we were Canadian before all things, and then we commenced to sing Canadian national songs. Old favorites received a new lease of life and became more popular than ever, and then in quick succession came new favorites and added fresh fuel to the patriotic fire. No one will, we think, deny that the singing of these patriotic songs by great bodies of voices throughout the country was a potent factor in the immense growth of national sentiment during the past year. We make this digression as a tribute to the influence of music, even in its simplest forms, upon the national life.

NORMAL SCHOOL, TORONTO.

Musicians of the greatest culture and talent are to be found in every important Canadian centre men and women who have in many instances sacrificed their material prospects to the love of Art but we think it will be generally conceded that to the city of Toronto is due the honor of having been the first Canadian centre in which a broad and comprehensive system of musical education, through regularly organized institutions exclusively devoted to music, was

ONTARIO PROVINCIAL BUILDINGS, TORONTO.

8

carried out. It was also the first city to encourage the influx of first-class outside talent by the offer of really liberal permanent salaries to organists and choirmasters. Such musicians are now well paid everywhere in Canadian cities, but Toronto was undoubtedly the pioneer in this direction.

To-day Toronto probably possesses more large and well-equipped institutions for teaching music than any three Canadian cities, and the number of artists who make a first-class living within her borders either as virtuosi or teachers is a constant source of wonder to our visitors. Premising that these facts are fairly well known, we take it for granted that a brief description of the institutions, and sketch of the artists, who have made Toronto musically famous may be welcomed by our readers.

We have endeavored in this little work not only to present portraits of

INTERIOR OF MASSEY MUSIC HALL.

most of the persons whose careers are therein sketched, but to also present excellent engravings of nearly every institution which is at all associated with the teaching of music or the granting of musical degrees. This will give the work an added value as a souvenir and will ensure its preservation.

Let us say at the outset that Toronto was particularly fitted in many ways to become the musical centre of Canada. It had an initial advantage inasmuch as it was already the seat of most of the great homes of learning in Law, Medicine, Theology and the Arts, as well as being the seat of Provincial Government. One guarantee of excellence for any large musical institution which might happen to be started lay in the security which is given by the local presence of a powerful daily press with an efficient staff

9

of musical critics pledged to faithful reports of musical events *as they are*, and not colored to suit the local prejudices which are forced upon news-papers in smaller cities. The musical critics of the Toronto press form an exceedingly able body, distinguished for musical discernment—always encouraging to modest effort, and freely outspoken to those who are more ambitious. The large population of the city also rendered possible and profitable the erection of capacious halls and large churches in which the works of the great Masters might be suitably rendered. All these advantages would have been missed in a smaller city, no matter how great the ability of the local musicians.

ST. GEORGE'S HALL.

Everyone is familiar with the graceful spire of St. James' Cathedral. The glorious nave and chancel of this venerable building have lately been enriched by a pipe organ by Warren, at a cost of about $20,000. The present organist and choirmaster is Dr. Ham, who succeeded the late Stocks Hammond, whose untimely death is still fresh in the minds of music-loving Torontonians.

The Metropolitan Methodist Church, with its grounds, occupies about three acres in the heart of the city, and its graceful tower and pinnacles are well shown in the adjoining cut. The body of the church forms one of the best auditoriums in the city and contains a very fine three-manual organ, which has been presided over by Mr. F. H. Torrington for over twenty-five years with conspicuous ability.

St. Andrew's Church (King St.) is not much used as a concert auditorium, but it possesses an excellent organ, which has been for many years in charge of Mr. Edward Fisher, under whose direction the choir has acquired a reputation all over the Province.

METROPOLITAN CHURCH, TORONTO.

Another church famous for the excellence of its music is the Baptist Church on Jarvis Street, of which Mr. A. S. Vogt is the efficient organist and choir-master. It is a question if the musical services of this church are not as famed as that of any in the Dominion. Sherbourne Street Methodist Church has also achieved musical note of late years owing to the frequent and excellent recitals given therein by the organist, Mr. Arthur Blakeley.

Of halls for public music performances Toronto has not only a sufficiency, but possibly an "*embarras de richesses.*" This was not always so, but of late years the number of new halls erected has been so large as to render many of them unprofitable. Massey Hall, from its enormous size, excellent acoustic qualities and central location, is easily the most important musical auditorium in Toronto or, for that matter, in Canada. Outside of R. C. churches or drill sheds, which latter are always uncomfortable and often bad acoustically, it is the largest auditorium in the Dominion, seating 3,000 people comfortably and accommodating an extra 1,000 if they are not particular as to comfort. The apparatus for heating in winter or lowering the temperature in summer is perfect. The decorations are sumptuous and the light abundant. It is scarcely necessary to tell our readers that this magnificent structure was the

SHERBOURNE STREET METHODIST CHURCH.

gift to the city of a single citizen, the late Mr. Hart A. Massey, who had the pleasure, while yet alive, of seeing his fellow-citizens enjoying the benefits of his munificence.

With the picturesque old Pavilion in the Horticultural Gardens everyone is familiar. It was till quite recently the auditorium *par excellence* of the city, but alas! with the advent of Massey Hall its glory has departed. It is still, however, used occasionally for important musical events.

St. George's Hall is an architectural and acoustic gem and exactly meets the requirements of those who intend to give small and select recitals amid artistic surroundings. Only those who have seen the hall can form an idea of its unique beauty. The idea is that of a Shire Hall, with stained glass windows, oak wainscoting, oak roof and roof timbers. Even the two fine Mason & Risch pianos with which the hall is equipped were specially finished in oak. The stained glass windows contain the armorial bearings of the various English counties, and in the daytime the effect from within is very beautiful. There are very fine halls in the buildings of the Y.M.C.A. and the Young Women's Guild, besides the very specially equipped halls in the Conservatory and College of Music, which will be mentioned elsewhere.

University College and Trinity College both grant musical degrees, and although Victoria College does not include music in its curriculum, it is the scene of many important and enjoyable musical events, and the beautiful chapel contains a very fine Mason & Risch organ. The architectural beauty of all three structures is so freely acknowledged that we have presented excellent cuts of them.

MR. F. H. TORRINGTON.

One of the first important steps toward the improvement of musical standards in Toronto was the action of the authorities of the Metropolitan Church in the year 1873 in securing the services of Mr. F. H. Torrington as organist of the new edifice. To those who know Mr. Torrington personally it is needless to say anything, but to those who have not that pleasure a few words may not be amiss. As organist and choirmaster of the Metropolitan Church, principal of the College of Music and conductor of the Orchestral School, he is one of the best known citizens of Toronto. This is owing to the fact, first, of his long residence here ; second, to his great musical ability, and third, to his still greater personal force of character. Since 1873 he has been a pillar of the Toronto musical fabric. As conductor of the Philharmonic Society, he has introduced most of the choral works of the great Masters to a Toronto audience for the first time. He has conducted festivals, organized societies, drilled orchestras and choirs, and organized musical institutions throughout an already long and eventful life, and has acted generally as "a planter of stakes" to show the musical path to a new

ORGAN OF METROPOLITAN CHURCH.

community. He is a man of wide musical culture and of the most unbounded energy. He never seems to rest.

MR. EDWARD FISHER.

There is a legend that he never sleeps, which, whilst believed by many, has never been fully demonstrated to be true. Mr. Torrington has always been a generous assistant to meritorious individuals or causes, frequently giving freely of his time and energy without hope of financial reward. In character he might be likened to some rugged, sturdy oak, the pioneer of the forest, under whose kindly sheltering branches many a younger tree has grown up to independence of support. Mr. Torrington toiled (as he still toils) with unflagging energy in the interests of Art. In the meantime the city had been steadily growing in population, wealth and culture, and with these came increased opportunity for men of mark in the profession. Six years after Mr. Torrington there came to Toronto Mr. Edward Fisher, who at once proceeded to identify himself with all that was progressive and artistic in the realm of music. Before coming to Toronto he had been connected with various prominent institutions and churches in other parts of the Dominion. He immediately assumed the post of organist of St. Andrew's Church and still fills the same position, and for twelve years acted as conductor of the Choral Society, a position which the increase of his professional duties compelled him to resign in 1891. His specialty in the profession is pre-eminently that of a teacher, having made the art and science of teaching, especially in its relation to the pianoforte, a constant study for

NEW HOME OF THE CONSERVATORY OF MUSIC.

many years. Mr. Fisher's most prominent characteristic is his unfailing and uniform courtesy. His interest in Art is unbounded, and his knowledge is as wide as his interest.

Early in the year 1886 Mr. Fisher conceived the idea of establishing an institution possessing the distinctive features of a European Conservatory of Music. In November of the same year the Toronto Conservatory of Music was an accomplished fact—the first of its kind in Canada and from that day to this it has continued upon its uninterrupted course of prosperity, and always under the direction of Mr. Fisher. For over eleven years the Conservatory occupied premises at the corner of Wilton Avenue and Yonge Street, but early in 1897 the constantly increasing business of the institution rendered it imperative to move into newer and more commodious quarters.

Ground was purchased at the corner of College Street and Queen's Avenue, a most commanding situation, within a stone's-throw of the Ontario Parliament Buildings. With such expedition were the new buildings erected that most of the rooms were ready for occupation before the commencement of the fall season of the same year. The new home of the Conservatory includes the largest and most completely equipped Conservatory buildings in Canada. The group consists of a main building, having a frontage of about fifty feet on College Street and extending south a distance of sixty-six feet, with a further extension of thirty feet beyond that immediately south of the main building, and adjoining the thirty feet extension is the Music Hall, forty-two feet wide and seventy-two feet long, running easterly towards Queen's Avenue. Extending well to the east of the main building, it forms with it a semi-quadrangle, upon which the doors of both buildings open. On the ground floor of the main building are situated the offices, reception-rooms, and main corridor, on one side of which is a large lecture hall, and on the other a suite of rooms for the musical director. At the rear are located a bicycle-room and lavatories.

On the next floor are located thirteen class-rooms and ladies' lavatory. On the next or top floor are seven class-rooms, and a hall which has been

ST. ANDREW'S CHURCH (KING STREET).

14

specially designed for the purposes of the Elocution School. All the rooms are well lighted and of ample size for the purposes required. Electric time bells are in every room, and speaking tubes at various points, all connected with the office ; double floors, partitions and doors have been constructed throughout, isolating the rooms respecting sound, adapting them to the requirements and comfort of both pupil and teacher. The Music Hall is somewhat unique in character. At the western end is the platform, which is adjoined by the retiring-rooms for performers. At the opposite end is a commodious gallery, reached by stairs direct from the auditorium. The main floor of the auditorium is in part level, to permit of its use for examinations and other purposes, while the portion toward and beneath the gallery rises in low steps, giving from all parts a good view of the platform and large Conservatory organ, which was remodelled and converted into a thoroughly modern electric organ, before being rebuilt into this new hall. The interior of the Music Hall is finished in buff pressed brick, having a high wood dado, and an artistically modelled plaster frieze consisting of cherubic figures dancing and performing on musical instruments. The roof, which is carried on boldly designed principals, is open to the ridge, and beautifully finished in unique panelled work. The buildings throughout are heated by steam and lighted by electricity and gas, especial attention being given to ventilation and sanitary conditions. The style of architecture is Italian in type, with accentuated angles in brickwork of two shades, and broad overhanging eaves. The buildings have been designed and superintended by Messrs. Burke and Horwood, who are well and favorably known as the architects of many prominent buildings in Toronto and elsewhere.

It is needless to say that the faculty of the Conservatory is a strong one. Detailed biographical sketches and portraits will be found in the alphabetical section of this book. The Conservatory is fully equipped with pianos by Chickering of Boston, Mason & Risch and other makers. The fine three-manual organ in the Concert Hall is by the Karn-Warren Company.

In the meantime Mr. F. H. Torrington had been steadily working for the advancement of music with that phenomenal energy which has ever been his most prominent characteristic. The activity of his musical life in this country may be shown by the numerous list of orchestral and choral works given under his direction by the Toronto Philharmonic Society and the Festival Chorus Orchestra. We have no space in this brief sketch to give a list of these works ; suffice it to say that such a list would comprise most of the great works written for such societies, and none of which could have been performed except under a leader of the very highest ability and culture.

Another of Mr. Torrington's prominent characteristics is his versatility. There are few orchestral instruments with which he his not familiar. He has lived so long amongst us that it will perhaps be news to the present generation to state that while residing in Boston he occupied the position of organist and musical director at King's Chapel, and was also conductor in association with Karl Zerrahn and the late P. S. Gilmore of the mass rehearsals of the great chorus of the last Boston Jubilee. He was also professor of piano and solo organist at the New England Conservatory of Music, first violin of the Harvard Symphony Orchestra, solo organist at Boston Music Hall, and solo organist at Plymouth Church, Brooklyn, N.Y.

After his removal to Toronto the same boundless energy and versatility were brought into play by him, and about 1888 Mr. Torrington organized and founded the Toronto College of Music and Orchestral and Organ School. The College is in affiliation with the University of Toronto, and has occupied from the first commodious and handsome premises on

COLLEGE OF MUSIC, TORONTO.

Pembroke Street, one of the handsomest thoroughfares in the city. There is a fine hall in the building, furnished with a Warren pipe organ, whilst the teaching and practice rooms are plentifully supplied with upright pianos by Mason & Risch and other makers. The College possesses an excellent library, and the office rooms are both comfortable and suitable to their purpose. Having given a very fully description of the building in our last issue, it is unnecessary to repeat it here, suffice it to say that the institution is considered by the most eminent authorities in England (who are well acquainted with its work) to be second to none in this country. That the staff of the College is of the highest character goes without saying. The name of the Principal is almost a household word, whilst a reference to the alphabetical section of this book will show that many of the most prominent artists in the city are also connected with the various departments of the institution.

The Metropolitan School of Music (1494-96 Queen Street West, Toronto) is one of the most promising of the teaching institutions which have sprung into being in Toronto within the last few years. From its inception financial matters have been handled by a Board composed of many of the most prominent financiers in Toronto, whilst its business administration has been in charge of the secretary, Mr. Edmond L. Roberts, Toronto correspondent of the *New York Musical Courier*. While financial assistance is indispensable at the start of any musical institution, the permanent success must, however, depend upon the qualifica-

tions of the musical executive. Mr. W. O. Forsyth, principal of the Metropolitan School of Music, is a musician of superior talent, a pre-eminently fine teacher of pianoforte playing, and an excellent harmonist. He is a composer of distinction, having written many delightful pianoforte morceaux, a prelude and fugue for organ, and some charming songs, and is also the author of some important orchestral works. So much for his versatility.

After early training in Toronto and elsewhere, Mr. Forsyth studied in Germany at the Leipzig Conservatory and privately with the eminent masters, Martin Krause, Jadassohn, Adolf Ruthardt, Bruno Zwintscher and Richard Hofmann, of Leipzig, and Julius Epstein, of Vienna.

Mr. Forsyth writes on musical matters in a way to command attention, which probably explains the fact that he is a paid contributor to three of the large musical journals in the United States. With a principal of this calibre, and a faculty also selected with the greatest care and judgment, it is little wonder that the Metropolitan School has made a mark for itself in the world of musical progress. It may be mentioned further that the School was especially established to fill the long-felt need of an institution of that kind in the west end of the city which would obviate the necessity of making long and frequent trips to the older up-town schools. The foresight of its founders has received ample justification in the sudden and surprising growth of the attendance. It has a sure and brilliant future before it. The School is fully equipped with Mason & Risch and other pianos, and occupies a handsome structure on the leading thoroughfare of Parkdale.

METROPOLITAN SCHOOL OF MUSIC.

Among the Canadian musicians who came into special prominence about this time, through the excellence of their work, was Mr. A. S. Vogt, the well-known and successful organist and choirmaster of Jarvis Street Baptist Church. Mr. Vogt's early musical education was obtained in this country. In 1882 he spent a year in the New England Conservatory of Music, Boston, and from 1885 to 1888 was a pupil of the Royal Conservatory of Music of Leipzig, Germany. In 1888 he came to Toronto, accepting the important position of choirmaster at the Jarvis Street Baptist Church, the leading church of the denomination in Canada (a cut of

MR. A. S. VOGT.

which appears here), the choir of which, under his direction, has earned a reputation for its excellence which has extended far beyond the boundaries of our own Province.

As a teacher of the piano—a sphere of work in which he specializes—his

JARVIS STREET BAPTIST CHURCH.

success is best shown by the prominence attained by many of his pupils, both as public performers and instructors of music. He is engaged as a piano instructor at the Conservatory of Music, Moulton Ladies' College, and at Mrs. Neville's and Miss Dupont's schools for young ladies. Many of his organ pupils are occupying leading positions in the city and various parts of the Province.

ORGAN OF JARVIS STREET BAPTIST CHURCH.

18

Of recent years his name has been associated as conductor with the Mendelssohn Choir of Toronto—a vocal society the fame of which has travelled beyond the borders of Canada. Mr. Vogt is among the most energetic and busily occupied of Canadian musicians. His success is due to those sterling qualities which are never slow to assert themselves, and which ever find ready recognition at the hands of a discriminating public. Mr. Vogt is also one of the most prominent of Canadian musical critics and his articles in the public press of Toronto are always read with interest. In this sphere of work he wields an influence which it would be difficult to estimate.

## THE GREAT LADIES' SCHOOLS OF TORONTO.

Miss Veals' Ladies' School, Glen Mawr, one of the large and well-established schools of Canada, is widely known for its high moral tone and for its thoroughness in scholastic work. It combines all the refinements and comforts of a good home with the best educational advantages. Glen Mawr is pleasantly situated in an open and healthy part of the city, and is within five minutes' walk of the University Buildings in the

MISS VEALS' SCHOOL, GLEN MAWR, TORONTO.

Queen's Park. The department of music is an important one, the faculty being exceptionally strong and including such well-known names as the following: Miss C. A. Williams, piano and singing; Miss Hillary singing; Miss Graham, piano and singing; Fraulein Rahtjen, piano; Miss Archer, violin; Herr Wiehmayer, piano; Mr. Forsyth, piano; Mr. Harrison, piano; Mr. Baumann, violin. The music department is equipped with ten pianos, nine of which are by Mason & Risch.

GARDEN ENTRANCE, GLEN MAWR.

Havergal Ladies' College was opened as "Havergal Hall" in September, 1894. From the outset, the College has been strikingly successful.

HAVERGAL LADIES' COLLEGE, TORONTO.

Seventy-six pupils received instructions during the first year, and in the fourth year the number was about 145. To meet the increasing demand for accommodation three adjoining houses have been leased, in addition to the original school building. Permanent premises having now become necessary, a large piece of land has been purchased on Jarvis Street, north of the present houses, and by next September entirely new buildings will be erected. The musical department is an important one, and the faculty includes such teachers of eminence as Herr Wichmayer (a pupil of Martin Krause, of Leipzig), Mr. A. S. Vogt, Dr. Saunders and Mr. W. Robinson. The first two gentlemen attend to the instrumental department, and the last two to the vocal branch. The College is fully equipped with pianos, about half being by Mason & Risch.

The institution is one of the most flourishing of its kind in the city. Several members of the resident staff, including the principal, Miss Knox (Oxford), have had the unusual advantage of training in the great Universities of England, Scotland and Canada.

Bishop Strachan School (Miss Grier, principal) is one of the oldest ladies' colleges in the Province, and occupies a most

BISHOP STRACHAN SCHOOL, TORONTO.

interesting structure on College Street. Its general educational character is too well known to need attention at our hands. We confine ourselves to the department of music, which is under the direction of Mr. J. W. F. Harrison, who is in turn ably supported by Miss Williams, Miss Frances Morris, A.T.C.M., Miss Ethel Morris, Fellow of Toronto Conservatory of Music, Miss M. M. S. McCarroll, A.T.C.M., Miss E. H. Mockridge and Mr. Baumann (violin). The musical education here given is of the most thorough. The School owns twelve pianos, all by Mason & Risch.

Mrs. Neville's Private Ladies' School, beautifully situated in park-like grounds corner of Bloor Street West and Avenue Road, is one of the most

MRS. NEVILLE'S RESIDENTIAL SCHOOL.

exclusive and select educational establishments in Canada, and has been in existence for nearly thirty years. Music has always been given a prominent place in the curriculum, such eminent artists as Frederic Boscovitz and F. H. Torrington having given instructions therein. At the present time Mr. A. S. Vogt and Miss Nora Hillary are in charge of the instrumental and vocal departments respectfully, assisted by Miss Williams, Miss Dallas, Miss Mockridge and Mr. W. E. Haslam. The department is equipped with a fine American grand and several Mason & Risch pianos.

The Toronto Presbyterian Ladies' College was founded in 1889 and incorporated in 1895 under the auspices of the Presbyterian Church. The following are the principal officers: President, Mrs. T. M. Macintyre; principal, Rev. J. A. MacDonald; lady principal, Miss Margery Curlette; registrar, William Houston, M. A.

The College is situated on Bloor Street West, facing the large open space which includes the Parliament Buildings, the University of Toronto and the majority of the great colleges of the Province. The general education given therein is most thorough, but we restrict ourselves to a consideration of the department of music. This department is carried on in connection with the Toronto Conservatory of Music, an arrangement which secures for students of this College exceptional advantages in the prosecution of their musical studies, including the services of a teaching faculty of over fifty members, and the benefit of a programme of work systematically arranged, and regularly tested from time to time by means of suitable examinations under the supervision of the director of the Conservatory. Students have the option of taking the full course to graduation, or of receiving the Conservatory certificates for the completion of the work prescribed in the various years.

PRESBYTERIAN LADIES' COLLEGE, TORONTO.

St. Margaret's College is one of the most recent additions to the teaching institutions of the city, having been founded in the fall of 1897. The buildings occupied by the College are spacious and well situated at the corner of Spadina Avenue and Bloor Street West. An extension of these premises is to be made at an early date. The education given is broad and comprehensive and includes an optional course of music under the best of local teachers. Connected with the music department are Messrs. Wiehmayer, Vogt, Jeffers, Ruth, Saunders, Robinson, Baumann and Hahn and Misses Alice Cummings, Gunther, Smart, Hessin and Davies. The recital of these names is equivalent to saying that the musical education is first-class. The College is in a thriving condition and is rapidly outgrowing its capacity, hence the projected addition to the buildings.

ST. MARGARET'S COLLEGE, TORONTO.

# Biographical Sketches.

### ❦ ❦ ❦

We will now turn our attention to a few biographical sketches of the artists who have helped to create musical Toronto. For ease of reference they are arranged alphabetically.

MRS. DRECHSLER ADAMSON, who so frequently delights Toronto audiences with her violin playing, is a daughter of Scotland, being born in Edinburgh, although a large portion of her life was spent in the German Fatherland. The early part of her musical education was received in Anhalt-Dessau, but she finally took up her abode in Leipzig, where her education was finished under the celebrated Ferdinand David. While in Leipzig she had the unusual honor of playing at the Gewand-Haus concerts.

Mrs. Adamson teaches violin and stringed instruments generally, at the Conservatory of Music. She is directress, also, of the celebrated Toronto String Orchestra, a combination of thirty pieces, which was established by her over three years ago, and which still maintains a vigorous existence.

Mrs. Adamson and her charming family (all of whom have embraced the musical profession) are amongst the most welcome performers upon the Toronto musical platform.

MRS. DRECHSLER ADAMSON.

MR. J. HUMFREY ANGER, the well-known Professor of Harmony and Counterpoint at the Toronto Conservatory of Music, has had a distinguished career as a musician. He was born in Berkshire, England, in 1862. His first appointment was as organist and choirmaster of the parish church of Frenchey, near Bristol. Whilst there he won the gold medal offered by the Bath Philharmonic Society for the best cantata for solo voices, chorus and orchestra; the judges being Sir Arthur Sullivan, Dr. A. C. McKenzie, and Eaton Fanning.

Mr. Anger is a Mus. Bac. of Oxford. He is also a F. R. C. O. of England, and has held the following positions: Organist of Ludlow Church, Shropshire, England; conductor of the Ludlow Choral and Orchestral Society. In 1892 he was elected a member of the Incorporated Society of Musicians. Shortly after his appointment to the Professorship at the Conservatory of Music, in 1893, he was made one of the examiners in Music for Trinity University, which position he still holds. He has given several organ recitals in Toronto, in addition to fulfilling his other onerous duties. Under his direction the Philharmonic Society has successfully rendered several of the great choral works, including "The Messiah," "Creation," and Rossini's "Stabat Mater."

MR. J. HUMFREY ANGER.

MISS KATE ARCHER is a native of Toronto. At the age of seven she commenced the study of the piano, and two years later was placed for violin instruction under

Mrs. Adamson, with whom she remained for some years, subsequently studying violin and harmony with Mr. Arthur E. Fisher, Mus. Bac. She has taken a scholarship, silver and gold medals for harmony at the Conservatory of Music, and silver medal at Trinity College, Toronto, where she obtained her Mus. Bac. degree at the early age of twenty. Miss Archer has also had violin lessons from Miss Mary S. Grassick, who was a pupil of such celebrated masters as Schradieck of Leipzig, Marsick of Paris, and Henry Holmes, director of the Royal College, London, England. Miss Archer has been very successful both as concert violiniste and as a teacher, having taught in the last few years (in addition to private pupils) with Miss Veals, Mrs. Neville, and Bishop Strachan School. She is the sole teacher of violin and harmony in the Ontario Ladies' College, Whitby.

MISS KATE ARCHER.

MR. JOSEPH CHURCHILL ARLIDGE, who for the past twelve years has been one of the most distinguished flautists on the Canadian concert platform, was born in the classical town of Stratford-on-Avon, England. He was educated under such famous masters of the flute as Antonio Minasi, Benjamin Wells, and Geo. Rudall. He also studied theory, piano and organ for two years under Lemmens. His talent was most precocious, and he made his first appearance as a flute soloist in the year 1859 at the early age of ten. This was at the Crystal Palace, under the famous Sir Julius Benedict, and he played an obligato for Mme. Parepa Rosa. This lady he also accompanied on subsequent tours, also Mme. Lemmens Sherrington. He came to Canada in 1885, and with a few years' exception has resided in Toronto ever since. For some years he was organist and choirmaster at Carlton Methodist Church, and is at present organist at Christ Church, Deer Park.

MR. JOSEPH CHURCHILL ARLIDGE.

MR. JOHN BAYLEY.—Thousands will instantly recognize the portrait which we herewith present of Mr. John Bayley, bandmaster of the Queen's Own Rifles, a position which he has held since 1879. The band is one of the most famous in Canada, and its efficiency is entirely due to this gentleman, who is as popular as he is able. Before assuming his present position Mr. Bayley was bandmaster of Her Majesty's 46th Regiment (Imperial Army). As to the efficiency of the Q. O. R. Band, it is sufficient to remind our readers that in the recent band competition at Hamilton it took the prize over all competing bands.

Mr. Bayley is an excellent violinist and orchestral leader, and teaches in both of these branches in the Toronto Conservatory of Music. He is a pupil of the celebrated Jansa, who was also the teacher of Madame Norman Neruda. Mr. Bayley helped to organize the celebrated Monday popular concerts,

MR. JOHN BAYLEY.

which delighted Torontonians for so many years in the old Pavilion, and which were only discontinued owing to the fact that so many of his associate artists eventually left the city.

24

BAND OF QUEEN'S OWN RIFLES.

MR. ARTHUR BLAKELEY'S name is so closely identified in the public mind with the idea of particularly agreeable organ recitals given upon the fine organ of the Sherbourne Street Methodist Church, that it is difficult to realize that things were ever very different. Mr. Blakeley, however, is a comparatively young man. He came of a distinguished musical family in the city of Leeds, England. He is one of the most prominent of the younger Canadian musicians. He has made a specialty of church music, and became a professional organist at the age of twelve. He came to Canada in the year 1884, and has since made Toronto his home. He presided for some time at the organ of the Church of the Ascension. Subsequently (in 1886) he received the appointment of organist of Sherbourne Street Methodist Church, which position he still occupies. The musical service of this church shows marked evidence of care and thought, and the attainments of Mr.

MR. ARTHUR BLAKELEY.

Blakeley as an organist may be judged from a reference to it. As a concert organist Mr. Blakeley has been a distinguished success; his monthly recitals have always been well attended, and he has been a prominent factor in popularizing the organ. That he is original and versatile is evident at a glance at any of his programmes. Since this article was first written Mr. Blakeley has also assumed the duties of choirmaster and has organized an excellent orchestra in connection with his church.

MR. H. M. BLIGHT.

MR. H. M. BLIGHT has for many years been one of the most welcome artists on the Toronto concert platform. He is the happy possessor of a high baritone voice of clear ringing quality. His versatility is very great, and he seems equally at home in oratorio or ballad singing. He is a native of the old city of Quebec, and received his early education in Canada, but afterwards studied under two famous masters, Lyman Wheeler, of Boston, and Signor Agramonte, of New York. He was for over ten years choirmaster of Elm Street Methodist Church, and now occupies the same position in Bloor Street Presbyterian Church, the musical services of which are unusually excellent. He is conductor of the Victoria Glee Club, and he is still open to receive engagements for concert work.

MRS. BLIGHT (wife of the above gentleman) is fully as well known as her husband, or together they have given joint organ and vocal recitals throughout Ontario. Mrs. Blight is a native of St. Catharines, where she originally studied organ playing under Mons. A. Gagnier, and subsequently under Messrs. F. H. Torrington, S. B. Whitely and others. She was for many years organist of Elm Street Methodist Church, and at the present time fills the same position with marked ability in the Bloor Street Presbyterian Church, where Mr. Blight is choirmaster. Apart from her work as a solo organist, Mrs. Blight enjoys a great reputation as a concert accompanist, either on organ or piano, and improvises and transposes at sight with great facility, two very great qualifications for an accompanist. She is also the author of several well-known sacred compositions.

MRS. H. M. BLIGHT.

27

MISS BESSIE BONSALL, the well-known contralto soloist, commenced the serious study of vocal music under Mr. W. E. Haslam in the Toronto College of Music in 1890. During the first year she won the Haslam Scholarship, and a special scholarship offered by St. James' Cathedral. Shortly after this she secured the position of contralto soloist in the Broadway Tabernacle, in New York City. This position she gave up in order to become a member of the celebrated concert troupe accompanying Ovide Musin, the great Belgian violinist. This engagement lasted two seasons. In 1895 Miss Bonsall decided to study abroad, and left for London, England, where she became a pupil of Mr. Charles Santley. Acting on the suggestion of several gentlemen eminent in music, she joined for a time the D'Oyley Carte Company at the Savoy Theatre with a view to acquiring a knowledge of stage methods. During this engagement she scored many successes. She is now at her old home in this city filling engagements for a short season, but will soon return to London, England.

MISS BESSIE BONSALL.

Among the resident professional musicians of Toronto, there are few who have taken a more active part in its musical life during the past twenty-five years than Mrs. S. R. Bradley. Her early studies in singing and piano were directed by Mr. Van Koerber, of Port Hope, and subsequently by Mr. John Carter and Mrs. Grassick. Her voice is a brilliant soprano and its striking qualities combined with an attractive style have won her great favor. At the age of seventeen she was entrusted with one of the principal solos at a public performance of "The Messiah" in Toronto. Since that time she has taken a prominent part in most of the great musical events of the city. She has been choir director of Berkeley Street Methodist Church for fourteen consecutive years and has taught for fifteen years in Whitby College. Many of her pupils are now filling positions as teachers and church soloists in Canada and the United States.

MRS. S. R. BRADLEY.

MR. W. J. A. CARNAHAN is one of Toronto's most popular baritones. Being gifted with a voice of exceptional power and refinement, which is held well under control, and further having an excellent stage presence, he has succeeded in making himself extremely welcome and popular in a very short space of time. Mr. Carnahan has sung in nearly every city and town in the Province, and has scored successes everywhere. He is a native of Meaford, Ont., and came to Toronto about ten years ago, and has since studied under Mr. Torrington, Mr. Haslam and Signor Tesseman. In addition to his stage work, Mr. Carnahan is one of the teachers of voice culture at the College of Music, and also acts as choirmaster of Emmanuel Presbyterian Church, East Toronto.

MR. W. J. A. CARNAHAN.

28

Mrs. S. CHADWICK, organist, pianist and concert accompanist, is a recent addition to Toronto musical circles.

This lady has had extensive experience in London, Ont., St. John, N. B., and Montreal, having been associated in the latter city as organist with Prof. Conture in Christ Church Cathedral and Trinity Church. Mrs. Chadwick was selected as accompanist for the concert tour of Mr. Ffrangcon Davies, the celebrated Welsh baritone, who so charmed the music lovers of Toronto, Ottawa, Montreal and London about a year since.

MRS. S. CHADWICK.

MR. A. T. CRINGAN, choirmaster of Cooke's Church, conductor of the Caledonia Choir, principal singing instructor in the Public Schools in Toronto, and teacher of sight-singing at the Conservatory of Music, is the most prominent Canadian exponent of the Tonic Sol-Fa system. He is a native of Scotland, and at the early age of twenty was appointed choirmaster of the Bloomgate U. P. Church in Lanark. In this position he made such a mark that he shortly afterwards gave up his ordinary business avocations and devoted himself entirely to the profession of music, which he has followed ever since. Before leaving Scotland he studied at the Tonic Sol-Fa College under Dr. W. G. McNaught, Mr. Jos. Proudman and Herr Emil Behnke, the eminent authority on vocal physiology. He passed the "exams" for degree of Mus. Bac. at Toronto University and came out first in 1897, and was presented with a gold medal by Mr. J. L. Hughes, Superintendent Public Schools, Toronto, as a memento of his graduating during the Diamond Jubilee year, 1897. Those who have had the pleasure of hearing the Public School children sing *en masse* at public festivals can bear testimony to the extraordinary success which has attended Mr. Cringan's efforts in this direction. He is a genial gentleman of a broad, sympathetic nature, and is beloved by the children, with whom he is so much brought in contact, and has the unlimited respect of the regular-line musicians who adhere to the old Staff system of notation.

MR. A. T. CRINGAN.

MRS. CHARLES CROWLEY, who made her professional *debut* a little over a year ago in Toronto, and who is already one of the most welcome of our platform artists, is a native of Canada. She commenced her studies under the best masters in London, England, and was a pupil for three years of Mr. W. Elliott Haslam in this city, and formerly of the National Conservatory of Music of America. Mrs. Crowley is possessed of a pure soprano voice of great brilliance, flexibility and compass. Her repertoire is varied and extensive, ranging from ballad to the most exacting and difficult *aria di bravura*. Mrs. Crowley has already appeared in many Canadian cities, and made a particularly favorable impression in Montreal when she appeared there in November, 1897.

MRS. CHARLES CROWLEY.

29

MISS SARA E. DALLAS.—Of the ladies who follow music as a profession in Toronto, Miss Dallas is one of the most brilliant. She was one of the first to obtain the degree of Bachelor of Music at Trinity University. For several years she has been organist of the Central Presbyterian Church, during nine of which she had also control of the choir. Miss Dallas has been connected with the Conservatory of Music and the Presbyterian Ladies' College since their organization, and was pianist for the Toronto Choral Society when most of the heaviest works were produced.

Miss Dallas is a brilliant example of how thorough a musical education can be obtained without going outside of Toronto, as she freely gives credit for the whole of her instructions on piano and organ to Mr. Edward Fisher, and for theoretical work to Mr. Arthur E. Fisher. Miss Dallas has been the recipient of several other musical honors and degrees, which we regret that we have not space here to enumerate.

MISS SARA E. DALLAS.

MR. ARTHUR L. E. DAVIES, the well-known baritone, was born in London, England, in 1867. He came to Canada in 1883, residing for a time in Montreal, where he assumed a position in Trinity Anglican Church in that city. In 1886 he came to Toronto and at once joined the choir of St. Mark's Church, Parkdale, which he left five years later to accept a position in Jarvis Street Baptist Church choir as solo baritone. He has a full, round, resonant voice, and being an exceptionally quick reader and gifted with a pleasing presence, he has become very popular as a church and concert baritone. His present position in the profession is due to personal energy in utilizing to the best advantage a voice naturally of fine timbre and quality. He, however, freely acknowledges his indebtedness for many points of style and expression to his friend, Mr. A. S. Vogt, the organist and choirmaster of Jarvis Street Baptist Church.

MR. ARTHUR L. E. DAVIES.

At present he devotes his time principally to directing the Toronto Male Quartette, one of Toronto's popular concert attractions.

MISS ALICE DENZIL, the well-known teacher of vocal music in the Conservatory of Music, came from England to Canada in the year 1881, specially to fill a position in the Ottawa Ladies' College, which at that time was one of the largest institutions of the kind in this country. This position she continued to fill for over eight years, when she moved to Toronto to join the staff of the Conservatory of Music, a position which she still holds. Miss Denzil is a pupil of the famous Mme. Sainton-Dolby, for whom Mendelssohn wrote the contralto part of his oratorio, "Elijah." Early in her career Miss Denzil earned the reputation of being one of the most conscientious and successful teachers of the vocal art in the Dominion, and this reputation she still sustains. She is the possessor of a rich contralto voice of rare purity, which she uses in the most artistic manner. Miss Denzil, apart from vocal work, is extremely versatile, has practical knowledge of orchestral instruments, and on one special occasion conducted comic opera with great success.

MISS ALICE DENZIL.

30

Mr. Adam Dockray, of the Church of the Redeemer, on Bloor Street West, enjoys the distinction of being probably the youngest choirmaster in the city. He was born in Toronto twenty-three years ago, and studied for voice under Mr. W. H. Robinson, of Toronto, and Messrs. H. Osborne and Edward Hayes, of New York. He also studied violin under Mr. Percy Mitchell and Herren Kuchenmeister and Klingenfeld, all of this city. He has, however, lately given almost all his attention to his vocal studies, and has recently spent a considerable amount of time in New York studying German opera under the most favorable auspices. That a gentlemen of his years should act as successor to the many prominent artists who have in the past directed the choir of the Church of the Redeemer is sufficient testimony to his ability. He is the possessor of an excellent tenor voice. He is studying for the degree of Mus. Bac. at Trinity University, and has successfully passed his first year.

MR. ADAM DOCKRAY.

Mr. Edgar R. Doward, organist of the Broadway Tabernacle, Toronto, is beyond doubt one of our ablest organists. He was born in Worcester, England, in 1850, and received his early training as a chorister in Worcester Cathedral, under the celebrated Dr. Doane. At the early age of thirteen he was appointed organist of the Whittington Church (named after the celebrated Dick Whittington, Lord Mayor of London), at seventeen, organist of the St. John's Church, Worcester, which appointment he left to take the appointment of Christ Church, Ottawa. He has also been organist (in Canada) of the following churches: Kingston Cathedral; St. Peter's, Cobourg; St. James' Cathedral, Toronto; Jarvis Street Baptist Church, and the Church of the Ascension, Toronto. In addition to his ability as a musician, Mr. Doward is one of the most affable and courteous of men. As to Mr. Doward's success *as a maker of organists*, it is sufficient to state that twenty-one pupils of his at present occupy positions as paid organists in the Province of Ontario.

MR. EDWARD R. DOWARD,

Mr. W. E. Fairclough belongs to a well-known English family, members of which have recently settled in Canada, and occupy positions of the greatest honor in Music, Literature, Art or Science. Mr. W. E. Fairclough is a Fellow of the Royal College of Organists, London, England, and ever since his arrival in Toronto has filled the position of organist and choirmaster at All Saints' Church in this city. He is also a musical director of the Hamilton Ladies' College, and teacher of organ, piano, and theory at the Toronto College of Music. He is distinguished as much for his great courtesy of manner and his personal popularity as he is for the other qualities on which his professional reputation rests. While Mr. Fairclough is one of the most unassuming of gentlemen in demeanor, he is considered one of the highest authorities in all that concerns organ playing or theory.

MR. W. E. FAIRCLOUGH.

31

MR. CECIL FORSYTH is a Canadian and was born near Aurora, Ont., and is one of the most promising juniors in the profession. He was educated for piano under his brother, Mr. W. O. Forsyth, and Mr. H. M. Field, and in harmony under his brother also. He is a member of the staff of the Toronto Metropolitan School of Music, where he teaches theory and pianoforte playing. He also lectures ably on musical history and musical form at the same institution.

MR. CECIL FORSYTH.

MME. LUCY FRANKLEIN is one of the most distinguished of our recent musical acquisitions. She is a native of London, England, and received her early education from Mr. Wallworth, chief professor at the Royal Academy of Music and Guild Hall College of Music, London, England; made her *début* at Covent Garden Theatre with Mme. Carlotta Patti, from whom she received great praise and encouragement; subsequently appeared in oratorio at Exeter Hall, in conjunction with Charles Santley and most of the illustrious singers of the day, with whom she travelled on concert tours throughout Great Britain; has also sung with great success the contralto *roles* in most of the principal operas with the celebrated Carl Rosa Opera Company, with which she was connected for several

MME. LUCY FRANKLEIN.

seasons. She subsequently came to Toronto on a visit, and Mr. Torrington, with his usual keen perception of talent, realized her possibilities and secured her services for the Toronto College of Music, with which institution she is now connected as a teacher of vocalization. She is the possessor of a magnificent contralto voice, and it is to be hoped that Toronto audiences will be favored by her appearance in public at an early date.

MR. PAUL HAHN, is a native of Stuttgart, Germany, where he resided during the first fifteen years of his life. During this period he seems to have liberally imbibed the musical spirit of his native land, for on his arrival in this city he was welcomed as a 'cello player of great talent and still greater promise. He has faithfully continued his studies upon his pleasing but difficult instrument, and is now always sure of a warm welcome from a Toronto audience. He is connected with the Toronto College of Music, where he is a teacher of violoncello and is a great favorite in the drawing-room.

MR. PAUL HAHN.

32

MR. HENRY HERBERT GODFREY, whose portrait appears here, claims to be neither a professional musician nor a literary man. He is a business man first and a musical amateur afterwards, and his claim to a place here is based upon the very great popularity achieved by his patriotic Canadian songs. His "Land of the Maple" is a household word throughout Canada, and may be considered as one of our national songs. His "Men of the North," "The Homeland," "Story of the Flag," and "Hark! the Drum," are also fast gaining popularity. Mr. Godfrey disclaims any great artistic merit for his work and is satisfied with having reached the hearts of the people by simple methods of writing. How successful he has been in his efforts to increase patriotic fervor by means of his songs, may be understood when it is stated that over 77,000 copies *of the "Land of the Maple" alone* were issued within ten months from the date of first publication. The sale of this song and of "The Men of the North" and "The Homeland" constantly increases, and there are but few public gatherings at which at least one of them is not sung. Their general use in the Public Schools is a guarantee of their permanence. Mr. Godfrey is an Englishman, forty years of age, but has lived in this country since 1874, and so may be considered as a thorough Canadian. Mr. Godfrey writes the words as well as the melodies of his songs.

MR. HENRY HERBERT GODFREY.

MISS ANNIE HALLWORTH, A.T.C.M., vocal teacher at the Toronto Conservatory of Music, received her musical education under Mr. W. Elliott Haslam, Miss Norman Reynolds for voice, and Mr. Arthur E. Fisher for harmony, and is at present continuing her piano studies under Mr. Edward Fisher. Miss Hallworth has gained quite a reputation as a vocal instructor, her concert method of teaching having been most successfully shown in the singing of her pupils at the numerous recitals given under her personal direction. She was successful in winning the Norma Reynolds gold medal in 1893, and graduated at the Conservatory of Music in 1896.

MISS ANNIE HALLWORTH.

MISS LENA HAYES, the distinguished young violiniste, is a native of Canada and pursued her study of the violin at first under Mons. Francois Boucher, the well-known concert violinist, and subsequently under Signor Guiseppe Dinelli, of the Toronto Conservatory of Music. After much careful work and study with the last named gentleman, she finally graduated at the Conservatory in 1891 and for two years was engaged in concert work and private tuition. In 1893 Miss Hayes was appointed a teacher of violin in that department of Conservatory work, and in the same year as teacher on the Presbyterian College staff, both of which positions she still holds. She still continues to appear in concert work and is always sure of a good reception.

MISS LENA HAYES.

33

MISS MAY HAMILTON is one of the most promising of the younger musicians of Toronto. She is the daughter of J. C. Hamilton, Esq., barrister, of this city. She pursued her musical studies at the Toronto Conservatory of Music, where she obtained two organ scholarships, graduating with honors June, 1896, under Mr. Edward Fisher. In April, 1897, she became organist of Cooke's Church, which post she still fills with ability, and during the late convention of the World's W. C. T. U. acted as organist in Massey Hall. She has recently visited New York, where she continued the study of the organ, under Mr. S. P. Warren. Miss Hamilton is a member of the Toronto Conservatory of Music organ staff. She has also studied counterpoint, harmony and piano under the best masters, and is in great demand as an accompanist at leading concerts.

MISS MAY HAMILTON.

MR. J. W. F. HARRISON, organist of St. Simon's Church, Toronto; musical director of the Ladies' College at Whitby; lecturer and teacher of advanced pianoforte playing at the Conservatory, is personally one of the most popular and prominent of the brilliant Englishmen who have made musical Toronto their Mecca. Mr. Harrison was originally engaged in London, England, to come to Canada as organist of St. George's Church, Montreal, whence he subsequently removed to Ottawa to fill the posts of musical director of the Ottawa Ladies' College, organist of Christ Church, and conductor of the Ottawa Philharmonic, which society performed, under his direction, many of the great choral works, such as "Creation," "The Messiah" (three times), "The Hymn of Praise," and "Elijah."

Mr. Harrison has resided for over ten years in Toronto, and long ago made himself one of the most popular of the teaching fraternity. His specialty is advanced pianoforte playing, and the large number of brilliant pianists throughout the Dominion whose education was finished with him testify to the thoroughness of his work.

MR. J. W. F. HARRISON.

MISS ADA E. S. HART.—Probably the most talented lady virtuoso in Canada is a native of Picton, Ont. She studied three years in the Ottawa Ladies' College under Mr. J. W. F. Harrison, where she took a gold medal for pianoforte playing. In 1891 she went to Leipzig, where she studied under Martin Krause for one year, and then went to Vienna, where she studied for three years under Leschetizsky, the famous teacher of Paderewski. On her return to Canada she made several brilliant tours, which won her golden opinions on every appearance. At the present time she is occupied with constant engagements and pianoforte teaching. Her technique is wonderful, her taste delicate, and her repertoire most varied and extensive. It is difficult to express sufficient appreciation of her great talents. Her reputation is bound to extend and grow, and she deserves all the success she may win, for few Canadians have studied so long or so persistently abroad, or under so great an artist as Leschetizsky. Miss Hart has also made a marked social success and entertains charmingly.

MISS ADA E. S. HART.

34

DR. ALBERT HAM, organist and director of the choir at St. James' Cathedral, and director of music at Upper Canada College, is one of the latest additions to our musical fraternity, but by no means the least distinguished. This gentleman was born in the historic city of Bath, England, and began his musical career as a choir boy at nine years of age; was for five years solo chorister at Church of St. John Baptist, Bathwick, and was two years later appointed sub-organist at the same church. In '92 he went to Taunton, where he filled the post of organist and director of the choir of St. John Evangelist, the most important musical church appointment there. During his five years' stay in Taunton he was conductor of the Taunton Choral Society, the Taunton Madrigal Society, and was local scholarship examiner for the Royal College and Royal Academy of Music up to the date of his leaving England. He has been highly

DR. ALBERT HAM.

successful as teacher of voice production. Mr. Douglas Powell, who recently made such a success in the Melba concert party, studied with Dr. Ham for two and a half years. As a "coach" in examinations his services were in much request. Amongst the latest distinctions in 1896 and 1897 gained by his pupils were three first Mus. Bac., Oxford; two F.R.C.O., London; two each A.R.C.O., London; A.R.C.M., London (singing and theory), and Lic. R.A.M., London (piano). His own degrees and diplomas obtained by himself are Mus. Bac., Trinity College, Dublin; Fellow Coll. Organists, London; Licentiate in Music, Trinity College, London.

MISS MINNIE F. HESSIN is a teacher of vocal music at St. Margaret's College, Havergal Ladies' College, and is noted as the possessor of a fine contralto voice of remarkable depth and power, which is very often heard on the concert platform or in the excellent choir of the Church of the Redeemer, in which she holds the post of contralto soloist. This lady is a native of Toronto, where she received instructions in the vocal art under Messrs. Haslam and Robinson, and in piano playing from Herr Wichmayer. Miss Hessin also took lessons for some time in New York from Mr. Edward Hayes, the famous voice specialist. Miss Hessin makes a specialty of concert and oratorio work.

MISS MINNIE F. HESSIN.

MR. V. P. HUNT received his musical education principally at the Leipzig Conservatory of Music, and after spending three years with the distinguished masters, Reinecke, Papperitz, Zwintscher, and Jadassohn, settled in Toronto, and for the past eleven years has been actively connected with the musical life of the city, and enjoys the reputation of being a most thorough and painstaking teacher. His specialties are piano, organ, and theory. His pupils come from all parts of Canada, and many of them now hold good positions as organists and piano teachers. He is teacher of piano at the Toronto Conservatory of Music, musical director of Demill

MR. V. P. HUNT.

Ladies' College, St. Catharines, and organist and choirmaster of the Central Presbyterian Church, in this city.

MR. W. ELLIOTT HASLAM.

MR. W. ELLIOTT HASLAM, singing master and conductor, who, although well known in Toronto, has a more than Canadian reputation, is a son of John Haslam, at one time a famous English baritone singer. He was first educated at the Royal Academy of Music, London, England, and afterwards under the elder Mazzucato, the last famous Italian "Maestro di Canto"; passed three years in Paris teaching and studying the French *roles* of operas; came to New York at the request of Vianesi; was brought to Toronto, where he established the Vocal Society, which gave twelve concerts with artistic and financial success; was six years musical director of St. James' Cathedral; returned to New York in '92, where he followed Fursch-Madi as Professor of Singing at the New York College of Music; the year after was appointed Professor of Oratorio at the National Conservatory of America, Dr. Anton Dvorak publicly speaking of the work of his class in the highest possible terms. Has formed successful singers and teachers in England, France, United States.

MISS NORA H. HILLARY, a most prominent vocalist and teacher of vocal culture, was born in Dublin, Ireland; came to Canada at an early age and studied piano in Toronto under Mr. Carl Peiler. Subsequently she revisited Dublin and studied under the famous Sir Robert Stewart, from whom she also received instructions in harmony, and from whom she doubtless received that deep and lasting groundwork and knowledge which has made her one of the most accomplished theoretical musicians in the city. Miss Hillary also received instructions at various times from Moderatie, of New York, and Manuel Garcia, of London, England. Accomplished a vocalist as Miss Hillary is, she still modestly declares that she has yet much to learn, as she never feels satisfied that the end has been reached. The teaching of voice culture is her specialty. She is one of the principal vocal teachers in the following ladies' schools: Mrs. Neville's, Miss Dupont's, Miss

MISS NORA H. HILLARY.

Veals', and St. Joseph Convent, and is also on the permanent staff of the Toronto College of Music. For seven years past Miss Hillary has conducted the Toronto Ladies' Choral Club with marked ability, and has taken an active and leading part in all musical matters.

MISS ETHEL HUSBAND.

MISS ETHEL HUSBAND, Mus. Bac., of the Toronto College, is one of the most successful of the college graduates, being an accomplished *ensemble* and solo pianist, as well as a Mus. Bac. University of Toronto. Miss Husband, who is a duly qualified teacher and member of the Toronto College of Music staff, studied the piano under Mr. Torrington and was prepared in the several branches of study at the Toronto College of Music. Miss Husband is a successful teacher and has a large class of pupils. She is but one of a very large number of accomplished and rising young musicians who own the College of Music as their Alma Mater and Mr. Torrington as their principal musical guide, philosopher and friend.

36

MISS AMY ROBSART JAFFRAY is a native of Ontario, and received her early musical education from Messrs. W. Elliott Haslam and E. W. Schuch, after which she went to Chicago and studied for three years under the famous Kowalski—three years of hard, laborious work. While in Chicago Miss Jaffray became a member of the well-known Chicago Ladies' Trio, and also acted as soprano soloist of Trinity Methodist Church, besides appearing in concert work with frequency. She returned to Toronto in the fall, 1897, when she joined the staff of the Metropolitan School of Music. In addition to this she has many private pupils, and devotes herself to teaching and concert work.

Miss Jaffray's voice is often referred to as a "mezzo"-soprano, probably because of its full timbre, which deceives the ear somewhat. Her voice is really a clear, high soprano. The excellence of Miss Jaffray's voice, the manner in which she uses it, and her pleasing stage presence combine to make her a favorite.

MISS AMY ROBSART JAFFRAY.

MR. T. C. JEFFERS.

MR. T. C. JEFFERS, Mus. Bac., has held the position of organist and choirmaster of the Central Methodist Church, Toronto, with distinguished success, for over eleven years, and has been a teacher of the pianoforte and organ, and lecturer at the Toronto College of Music from its commencement. He was one of the first to pass the numerous and comprehensive examinations required for the degree of Mus. Bac. at the University of Toronto, especially distinguishing himself in practical musicianship (playing), composition, and scoring for full orchestra. Mr. Jeffers' specialties are touch and style in piano playing, choir training, solo, organ and piano playing, accompaniment, theory, and voice training. In all of these branches his success as a teacher is evidenced by his numerous pupils who hold positions as teachers, choirmasters, organists and church and concert vocalists.

MR. PETER C. KENNEDY is a native of Scotland and started his musical career as a choir boy in Arbroath, and soon after travelled through Great Britain as a boy soloist, singing in St. Paul's Cathedral and other famous minsters on occasion. He came to Toronto in 1886 and studied under eminent local teachers. He is now a teacher of piano playing in the Metropolitan School of Music, where he also lectures on theory. He is also choirmaster and organist of St. Mark's Episcopal Church, Parkdale. A large proportion of his pupils took first prize at the last examinations of the Metropolitan School of Music, one of them winning the Mason & Risch scholarship for general proficiency.

MR. PETER C. KENNEDY.

37

MISS LILLIE KLEISER is a native of Dakota, but, having lived here from childhood, may be considered as a thoroughly naturalized Canadian. She is the possessor of a flexible soprano voice of an exceedingly pure quality, and is a great favorite with the Toronto musical public. She has a large and constantly increasing class of vocal pupils, and is a leading soprano in the choir of Sherbourne Street Methodist Church. While Miss Kleiser has demonstrated her ability as an artist, both in oratorio and operatic *roles,* she now confines herself to concert work and teaching. Her vocal training was received from Mr. E. Schuch, of this city, then from Mr. Henry Jacobson, of Buffalo, and finally Mr. Wm. Courtney, of New York. At the same time she studied piano playing under Messrs. A. S. Vogt and J. D. A. Tripp.

MISS LILLIE KLEISER.

MR. H. KLINGENFELD, solo violinist and teacher of violin at the Metropolitan School of Music, St. Joseph's Convent, Loretto Abbey, and Havergal Hall Ladies' Seminary, is one of our best known violinists, although but a recent comer among us. Mr. Klingenfeld hails from Munich, Germany, and studied with Abel and Benno Walter (Munich) and later at the Leipzig Conservatory under Schradick and Brodsky. From this celebrated institution he received a prize diploma acknowledging him to be one of the most talented and worthy pupils who had ever left the institution. He had the honor of playing in the orchestra of the Gewand-Haus concerts, and also in the celebrated Bayreuth Wagner Festival orchestra. After travelling for some time as a solo violinist in Germany, Sweden and Denmark, he crossed the Atlantic and made his abode in Halifax, subsequently moving to Toronto, where he has made a distinguished mark. Mr. Klingenfeld has made frequent appearances upon the concert platform in Toronto, and always with distinguished success.

MR. H. KLINGENFELD.

MRS. KLINGENFELD (wife of the above gentleman) is a favorite teacher of singing. She was born in Brooklyn, New York, and subsequently went to Berlin, Germany, where she merely studied music as an accomplishment. On her return, twelve years ago, she decided to follow a professional career, and again commenced her studies in Baltimore, under the most eminent masters. She is generally considered as a specialist in the branch of vocal music. She is gifted as an instructress, and has under her charge a very large class of pupils, who show forth the excellence of her method. Mrs. Klingenfeld's personal charm of manner has made her one of the most popular members of the profession in Toronto.

MRS. KLINGENFELD.

38

MRS. FRED. W. LEE, the well-known teacher of advanced piano playing at the Toronto College of Music, is a native of Toronto. She studied for some years at the College under Mr. H. M. Field, and has given several recitals which have elicited most favorable comment from the critics of the press, besides delighting the large audiences present. Mrs. Lee is possessed of the true fire of virtuosity; despite this, however, she has decided to devote herself to the art of pianoforte teaching. Later on, however, her friends hope to hear her again upon the concert platform. Mrs. Lee's class of pupils is a large one.

MRS. FRED. W. LEE.

MONS. FRANCIS X. MERCIER is a native of Bordeaux, France, and received first instructions in music from his father, who was many years tenor soloist at the Madeleine Church, Paris, France. He came to this country at an early age and became through hard study one of the most welcome of our platform singers. He is the possessor of a fine, pure, true tenor voice, and, having in addition a charming stage manner, he rarely fails to interest his audience. He came to Toronto about four years ago, and is well known in the Provinces of Ontario and Quebec. He has sung in grand opera in both New York and Boston. At the present time he is instructor in the vocal department of the Toronto Junction College of Music.

MONS. FRANCIS X. MERCIER.

MR. T. ARTHUR MILLER, who was born in 1879 in this city, is the youngest organist of Toronto, holding that position in the Carlton Street Methodist Church, which has for many years enjoyed a reputation for the excellence of its music. He studied organ for some years under Mr. Doward, and later under Mr. Vogt; piano under Miss Hart, and voice under Mr. Delasco. He assumed his first post (as organist of the Western Congregational Church) at the age of fifteen, and occupied it successfully for two years, when he assumed his present position. Mr. Miller is one of the most promising of our younger musicians.

MR. T. ARTHUR MILLER.

39

MISS EDITH J. MILLER.

MISS EDITH J. MILLER, whose fine contralto voice has so often charmed Toronto audiences, is a native of Portage la Prairie, Manitoba. She studied first in Winnipeg and afterwards in the Toronto Conservatory of Music, where she won a special gold medal on graduating. She also spent several months in Paris under Madame Marchesi, and in London under Alberto Randegger. Returning to Ontario, she filled several important engagements, and for a time occupied the position of contralto soloist in the choir of the Bloor Street Presbyterian Church. She has also taken several professional tours through Ontario and Manitoba and to the Pacific Coast. In the fall of 1897 she went to New York and pursued her studies under Mr. George Sweet. Early in 1898 she was appointed contralto soloist in St. Bartholomew's (Episcopal) Church, New York, and is booked for several important engagements in the East with oratorio societies and other musical organizations. Although she is thus temporarily exiled, she is still considered as one of Toronto's most favored singers, and her frequent re-appearance upon our concert platforms is earnestly hoped for.

MISS HELEN M. MOORE, who teaches harmony, counterpoint, canon, and general musical theory at the College of Music, Pembroke Street, studied theoretical work with Mr. A. E. Fisher, Mus. Bac., A. R. C. O., Eng., and the piano with Mr. H. M. Field; graduated from Trinity University in music in 1891; accepted and still holds a position in the Toronto College of Music, and has successfully prepared many pupils for the entire course of music at examinations held in Toronto University, as well as covering the entire theoretical course required for full graduation in Toronto College of Music.

MISS HELEN M. MOORE.

MISS BELLE HANDY NOONAN.

MISS BELLE HANDY NOONAN is the head of the elocutionary department of the Metropolitan School of Music. This lady is a native of Boston, Mass., in which home of learning she graduated from the Boston School of Expression, a famous institution which, by the way, was endowed by Sir Henry Irving. This graduation was the result of a three years' course in English literature, elocution, and physical culture. She came to Toronto in September, '97, and since then has been frequently heard from our public platforms, and has been always favorably received. Her press notices are uniformly flattering, and show the esteem in which she is held wherever she appears. The Boston Courier, one of the most responsible journals in Massachusetts, says: "She is by all odds the best reader in Boston." This is unusual praise.

MISS NORMA REYNOLDS, Professor of Singing at the Toronto Conservatory of Music, received her musical education under Mr. W. Elliott Haslam for the voice, Mr. H. M. Field for piano playing, and under Mr. Arthur E. Fisher for harmony; was for several years soprano soloist in several of the leading churches in Toronto, amongst others St. James' Cathedral and the Metropolitan Church; and is a member of the Arion Quartette. Miss Reynolds has, however, given her attention of late years exclusively to vocal teaching, and justly considers the success of her pupils her largest recommendation. Several concerts have been given exclusively by Miss Reynolds' pupils, and, although these entertainments were held in the largest halls in the city, the result was always an overflow of the audiences. We mention this simply as an evidence of Miss Reynolds' great popularity. Miss Reynolds prepares pupils specially for concert, church, and oratorio work, and has an ever-growing class.

MISS NORMA REYNOLDS.

MR. WM. F. ROBINSON, conductor of the University College Ladies' Glee Club, vocal instructor at the Toronto College of Music, Havergal Ladies' College, and St. Margaret's College, is a son of Mr. George R. Robinson, leader of the celebrated 13th Regiment Band of Hamilton, in which organization he held the position of solo clarinetist for several years. Mr. Robinson has only recently moved to Toronto, but has already met with great success in the field of vocal culture. He has had several years' experience as conductor of church choirs, choral and glee clubs, and is the possessor of a robust tenor voice, having studied with some of the most eminent singing masters, including Edward Hayes, principal of the School of Vocal Science at New York.

MR. WM. F. ROBINSON.

HERR RUDOLF RUTH.—This gentleman was born in Hanau, near Frankfort, in Germany; studied in Frankfort at Dr. Hoch's Conservatory for six years, and was a favorite pupil of Mme. Clara Schumann. He studied after this for two years in Brussels, where he played at several concerts, and subsequently travelled as a concert piano soloist in England, Scotland, and Belgium; came to New York in 1892, and subsequently came to Toronto under an arrangement with the College of Music. Subsequently he transferred his services to the Conservatory of Music and is still connected with this institution. Herr Ruth is a most accomplished pianist, and is also a violoncellist of ability. Since his arrival in Toronto Herr Ruth's time has been so completely taken up by pianoforte pupils that he has devoted no time to concert playing. His most special claim is that he is the sole teacher here of the Clara Schumann method, and that he is a teacher of the most thoroughly classical German style of pianoforte playing.

HERR RUDOLF RUTH.

MR. CHAS. E. SAUNDERS.

MR. CHAS. E. SAUNDERS, B.A., Ph.D., received his early musical training in London, Ontario. His later studies were carried on under various masters in Boston, New York, and elsewhere. He settled in Toronto about four years ago. Dr. Saunders has studied several branches of music, and has also acted as critic for various papers in Toronto, but of late he has confined himself to his specialty of voice training. He is a graduate of Toronto and Johns Hopkins Universities, at which institutions he received a thorough scientific education which has enabled him to deal, with unusual success, with the difficult problems of scientific voice production. In addition to his private class, he holds the post of vocal instructor at Havergal Ladies' College and St. Margaret's College.

MR. E. W. SCHUCH, whose genial countenance we here reproduce, has been for many years one of Toronto's popular baritone singers, and has figured largely in local concerts and oratorio performances. He is an excellent choirmaster, and for years filled that position in St. James' Cathedral and in the Church of the Redeemer. Mr. Schuch has shown a special tact in his handling of large bodies of amateurs, to whom his masterful manner gives confidence, and has acted as conductor with numerous local societies in the towns surrounding Toronto ; has also been conductor of the University Glee Club, Osgoode Glee Club, Harmony Operatic Club, and Toronto Vocal Society. Of late years he has devoted himself more to vocal teaching, and is at present instructor at the Loretto Abbey, having in addition a large number of private pupils.

MR. E. W. SCHUCH.

"SERANUS."

"SERANUS" is the *non de plume* of the talented artiste who in private life is known as Mrs. J. W. F. Harrison. Seranus has a dual artistic personality, for she is both a *litterateur* and a musician of distinction. Almost every one is familiar with her poetical works, but all are not aware that she is an accomplished musician, both in the creative and executive departments of the art. Her Canadian musical sketches, "Nocturne" and "Dialogue," are musical gems. Seranus has lectured frequently on "The Music of French Canada," and it is to be noted that both on the literary and musical side she has made a special study of French Canadians and their songs. Nor is this all, for this gifted lady is a prose writer of great merit, and articles from her pen have frequently appeared in the great magazines of England and the United States. The collection of poems by Seranus (published by W. Tyrrell & Co.), entitled "Pine, Rose, and Fleur de Lis," is one of the most readable books of Canadian verse extant. For versatility of talent it can certainly be said that she has no superior in Canada.

MR. H. N. SHAW, vocal instructor at the Conservatory of Music, is the son of an eminent vocal teacher in Boston. He has resided in Toronto for the last five years. He holds the degree of B.A. from the University of Acadia, N. S.; commenced his musical education in Boston, continued in New York, and later in London, England, Paris, Milan and Munich. Among the many teachers under whom Mr. Shaw has studied are Signor Agramonte, Herr Beyer, Wm. Shakespeare and Delle Sedie. Before coming to Toronto Mr. Shaw taught vocal music and elocution at Acadia University.

MR. H. N. SHAW.

MR. J. M. SHERLOCK.

MR. J. M. SHERLOCK is the possessor of a tenor voice of rare sweetness, and which he keeps under excellent control. He is a specialist in tone production, voice culture, and expression, and does a great deal of admirable work as oratorio tenor. He fills the positions of solo tenor with the Philharmonic Societies of Toronto, Hamilton, Berlin, Kingston, etc.; solo tenor at the Metropolitan Methodist Church, Toronto; singing master of the Metropolitan School of Music, and director and first tenor of the Sherlock Male Quartette (an organization noted for the finished character of its work, so much so that it is constantly in demand for public entertainments); was for two years solo tenor of the Sherbourne Street Methodist Church, Toronto. There are very few cities or towns in Ontario in which Mr. Sherlock has not made his appearance in concert work. The excellence of his teaching method is shown by the admirable way in which his pupils acquit themselves in public.

MISS HENRIETTA SHIPE is probably more frequently in demand as an accompanist than any other lady in the Toronto profession. To make a good accompanist requires a peculiar order of talent, and a degree of artistic self-effacement which is only too rare, and which, when found, is most highly appreciated by artists. Miss Shipe possesses these qualifications to an eminent degree, and hence her popularity in her special field of work. At the same time she is a solo pianist of great promise. She is a native of Cleveland, Ohio, and studied at the well-known Conservatory of Music at Oberlin, Ohio. She removed to Toronto in 1893 and has rapidly won public favor. As an accompanist she has been endorsed in flattering terms by so great an artist as Mr. Whitney Mockridge. At present she is organist of Jarvis Street Unitarian Church.

MISS HENRIETTA SHIPE.

MR. JOHN SLATTER.

MR. JOHN SLATTER, bandmaster of the 48th Highlanders' Band, is a well-known figure in Toronto. The picturesqueness of the dress of the Highland regiment made the band a favorite from the first, but its musical excellence is largely the work of Mr. Slatter, as he is a composer and arranger of merit, and is one of the finest instrumentalists in the country. He served for some years in H.M. First Life Guards' Band, of London, as a soloist, and more recently with the great Sousa. Mr. Slatter naturally feels very proud of his band, and aims to make it second to none in Canada.

MME. ADELE STRAUSS-YOUNGHEART is a native of the German Fatherland, and studied at the Conservatory in Strasburg, under Mme. Rucquoy-Weber, and in Paris, where she sang at concerts, and afterwards travelled through Europe. In New York she has sung with Messrs. Theodore Thomas and Damrosch, and has also appeared in many of the large American cities. She first came to Toronto in 1892, and has spent a considerable portion of her time here since, and is at the present time connected with the staff of the Toronto College of Music. Mme. Strauss-Youngheart is the possessor of a magnificent mezzo-soprano voice of wonderfully wide range. Her first appearance in Toronto was made with the Philharmonic Society in "Samson."

MME. STRAUSS-YOUNGHEART.

MISS FANNIE SULLIVAN, one of the most brilliant pianists in the Dominion, and decidedly the most talented *ensemble* artist of this city, is connected with the staff of the Toronto College of Music, where she teaches advanced pianoforte playing. She began her studies with the Sisters of Loretto; subsequently studied for a short time under the late Carl Martens, but finally became a pupil of Mr. F. H. Torrington, under whose direction she attained her present eminence. In '89 Miss Sullivan won the Torrington Organ Scholarship; in '90, the gold medal of the College for general proficiency, this being one of the most coveted distinctions sought for by Toronto students; in '91 she was the recipient of the Artists' Diploma and a special money prize for the best accompanist. Miss Sullivan has played with the Yunck String Quartette on several occasions in Toronto and Detroit, and as an artist makes a specialty of concerto playing with orchestra. In '93 she was appointed choir director of the Church of Our Lady of Lourdes, a position which she still holds, and under her direction this choir has rendered for the first time in Canada some of the best modern compositions, notably Silas' Mass in C and Dvorak's Mass in D. We look forward to a promising future from this talented young musician.

MISS FANNIE SULLIVAN.

44

BAND OF THE 48TH HIGHLANDERS.

MR. HOWARD STUTCHBURY is a native of Taunton, Somersetshire, England, where he received his early musical education. After his arrival in this country he continued his studies in the vocal art, under Mme. Sajous and Signor Vegara. Mr. Stutchbury is well known to Toronto concert-goers, possessing as he does a very pleasing high baritone voice, which he uses to the greatest advantage. Mr. Stutchbury acts as choirmaster and solo baritone of Parkdale Presbyterian Church, and is the director of the Parkdale Ladies' Glee Club. Before assuming his present duties at Parkdale, Mr. Stutchbury was for two years a baritone soloist in the choir of St. James' Cathedral.

MR. HOWARD STUTCHBURY.

MR. RECHAB TANDY, vocal instructor at the Toronto Conservatory of Music, is one of the leading oratorio and concert tenors of Great Britain and America. Mr. Tandy comes of a very musical family. He is an Englishman by birth, but came to Canada at an early age ; received his first musical instruction under John O'Neil, of the Boston Conservatory, and Signor Nuno, of New York. He finished his education under the celebrated Randegger, of London, England, and it is not therefore to be wondered at that Mr. Tandy is a master of the art of tone production, whilst his breadth of style and artistic finish mark all his efforts. In August, 1888, Mr. Tandy went to London, England. During his seven years' residence in that city he made frequent appearances at the celebrated Crystal Palace concerts, under the direction of August Manns, and followed his profession in London and throughout Great Britain with marked success. Mr. Tandy assumed his present position with the Conservatory about two years ago.

MR. RECHAB TANDY.

SIGNOR TESSEMAN is one of the most distinguished members of the profession in Canada. His coming here was of signal service to Canadian students in enabling them to study in the traditional Italian school of vocal art. As a boy he was trained in York Minster, together with Sir Joseph Barnby and Dr. Creser, afterwards organist and composer to the Queen at the Chapel Royal, St. James. His thorough training under the most eminent masters, added to his great ability and his association both on the operatic stage and platform with such artists as Patti, Nillson, Trebelli, Grisi, Sims Reeves, Mlle. Tietjens and Marimon, pre-eminently fitted him for the position he now holds, and ensures the advantages of Continental study to students. Signor Tesseman prepares singers for opera *roles*, in concert repertoire, oratorio and church work. He also bears most flattering letters of endorsation from such world-famous artists as Arditi, Wilhelm Ganz, Sims Reeves and Sir Arthur Sullivan.

SIGNOR TESSEMAN.

47

MR. JOHN WALDRON, the bandmaster of the 10th Royal Grenadiers, is one of the most popular members of the profession, and owing to the particular branch of it which he follows, his face is naturally very familiar to thousands who have had the pleasure of listening to his fine band when playing in the open air. Mr. Waldron is an Englishman, and before coming to Canada was for thirteen years bandmaster of the 1st Batt. of H.M. 8th Regiment (King's, Liverpool). He received his musical training at the Royal Military School of Music, Kneller Hall, and is a certificated instructor of all military band instruments and on military scoring. There is no question that the Grenadiers' Band has greatly improved under his direction, and to-day it has few equals in the Dominion.

MR. JOHN WALDRON.

MR. FRANK S. WELSMAN, the well-known solo pianist and teacher, began the earnest study of music at the Toronto College of Music, where for five or six years he studied piano, violin, theory and composition, gaining at the same time much valuable experience as an orchestral and quartette player. Mr. Welsman has recently returned from Germany, where he has been pursuing his studies for the last three years under such eminent masters as Martin Krause, Gustave Schreck, of the Royal Conservatorium, Leipzig, and Richard Hofmann. His testimonials and press notices show how highly he was esteemed as a musician by the masters and critics of Leipzig. Mr. Welsman has succeeded Mr. H. M. Field at the Toronto College of Music, and is also at the head of the theory department, a position which Mr. Welsman's natural ability and years of conscientous study eminently fit him to occupy.

MR. FRANK S. WELSMAN.

MR. THEODORE WIEHMAYER, one of Toronto's most prominent piano virtuosi and piano teachers, is a native of Prussia, and came to this country so recently as August, 1897. Mr. Wiehmayer studied for eight years at the Royal Conservatorium at Leipzig, three of which were passed under the personal direction of the famous master, Martin Krause. In 1890, Mr. Wiehmayer took an extended tour throughout Norway and Sweden, visiting nearly every city and town of importance and delighting all with his brilliant pianoforte playing. On this trip he accompanied one of the most distinguished of Swedish vocalists, and when we remember what artists hail from Sweden, this is saying a good deal.

Since his stay in Toronto, Mr. Wiehmayer has been busily engaged in forming and consolidating his teaching connection, and hence has not been heard so often as a concert virtuoso as his admirers would have liked. Those who have heard him speak of him in terms of the highest praise.

MR. THEODORE WIEHMAYER.

Mr. Wiehmayer teaches pianoforte playing at Miss Veals' School, Havergal College, and St. Margaret's College, in addition to a large private class at his studio, 53 Grenville Street.

48

BAND OF THE ROYAL GRENADIERS REGIMENT.

MR. FRED WARRINGTON, Toronto's ever-popular baritone, has lived so long in this city that it is difficult to realize that he is an Englishman born ; yet such is the fact. He studied for the voice under two of the most eminent teachers of the day, namely, Wheeler, of Boston, and Agramonte, of New York, who did all they could to improve an almost perfect voice. For twelve years Mr. Warrington has been choirmaster of Sherbourne Street Methodist Church, and for a still longer period he has figured in almost every concert of note in the city.

During the recent Jubilee performance of "Elijah," at Massey Hall, Mr. Berresford, who was to have sung the part of *Elijah*, was indisposed at the very commencement of the performance and had to retire whilst the concert was in progress. Mr. Torrington, the conductor, beckoned to Mr. Warrington, who was in the hall, and without a moment's hesitation he took up the *role* where Mr. Berresford had left off, and sang it through to the satisfaction and delight of the immense audience. This was done without the slightest preparation, and it is safe to say this performance constituted a *tour de force* which could have been accomplished by few artists in Canada.

MR. FRED. WARRINGTON.

Mr. Warrington has the Vocal Department at the Metropolitan School of Music, and his services may be secured for concerts for any part of the Dominion.

MISS C. A. WILLIAMS is one of the best known figures in musical society of Toronto, having given attention to vocal culture and pianoforte playing here continuously for the last twenty-two years. Miss Williams is a native of England, where she has studied under such distinguished artists as Herr Kuhe, Dr. Bennett and Signor Campana. Thirty-one years ago Miss Williams left England to join the staff of the Hellmuth Ladies' College, of London, Ont., where she remained four years and a half, and leaving there to come to Toronto, where she has ever since been professionally engaged, being connected with almost all the prominent teaching institutions of the city. This is apart from her private tuition. Miss Williams visits England every summer.

MISS C. A. WILLIAMS.

The sunlight gleams on murm'ring streams,
And sweetest melody
Pours from the feathered songsters in
The spreading maple tree.

--From "The Land of the Maple," by H. H. GODFREY.

# Toronto Directory of Musicians and Musical Institutions

### (Alphabetically Arranged)

ADAMSON, MRS. **DRECHSLER.** · · · · · 67 Bloor Street East
ANGER, J. H., · · · · · · 226 Jarvis Street
ARCHER, MISS **KATE.** · · · · · · 286 Huron Street
ARLIDGE, J. C., · · · · · 135 College Street
BAYLEY, JOHN, · · · · · 272 Sherbourne Street
BLAKELEY, ARTHUR, · · · · · 46 Phœbe Street
BLIGHT, HARRY, · · · · · · 40 Henry Street
BONSALL, MISS BESSIE, · · · · · 83 Hayden Street
BRADLEY, MRS., · · · · · 130 Seaton Street
CARNAHAN, W. J., · · · · · · East Toronto
CHADWICK, MRS. S., · · · · · 27 Bleecker Street
CRINGAN, A. T., · · · · · 633 Church Street
CROWLEY, MRS. GEORGE. · · · · · 383 Markham Street
DALLAS, MISS, · · · · · 99 Bloor Street West
DAVIES, A. L. E., · · · · · 158 Yonge Street
DENZIL, MISS, · · · · · Conservatory of Music
DINELLI, G., · · · · · 94 Gerrard Street East
DOCKRAY, ADAM, · · · · · 18 Mercer Street
DOWARD, E. R., · · · · · 112 Baldwin Street
FAIRCLOUGH, W. E., · · · · · 6 Glen Road
FORSYTH, C. C., · · · · · 212 Carlton Street
FRANKLEIN, MME., · · · · · 60 St. Patrick Street
HAHN, PAUL, · · · · · 147 Roxborough Avenue
HALLWORTH, MISS ANNIE, · · · · · Conservatory of Music
HAM, DR., · · · · · · 12 Carlton Street
HAMILTON, MISS MAY, · · · · · 86 Glen Road
HARRISON, J. W. F., · · · · · 13 Dunbar Road
HART, MISS ADA, · · · · · 1A Harbord Street
HASLAM, W. E., · · · · · 15 King Street East
HAYES, MISS LENA M., · · · · · 473 Euclid Avenue
HESSIN, MISS MINNIE, · · · · · 194 Bloor West
HILLARY, MISS NORA, · · · · · 9 Gloucester Street
HUNT, V. P., · · · · · 104 Maitland Street
HUSBAND, MISS ETHEL, · · · · · 509 Sherbourne Street
JAFFRAY, MISS A. R., · · · · · 1494 Queen Street West
JEFFERS, T. C., · · · · · 60 Isabella Street
KENNEDY, PETER, · · · · · 120 O'Hara Avenue
KLEISER, MISS LILLIE, · · · · · 36 Cecil Street
KLINGENFELD, H., · · · · · 494 Huron Street
LEE, MRS. FRED., · · · · · 111 Bloor Street West
MERCIER, F. X., · · · · · 259 Spadina Avenue
MOORE, MISS HELEN, · · · · · 20 Maitland Street
NOONAN, MISS BELLE, · · · · · 1494 Queen Street West
REYNOLDS, MISS NORMA. · · · · · 4 Pembroke Street
ROBINSON, W. F., · · · · · College of Music
RUTH RUTOLF. · · · · · 35 Grenville Street
SCHUCH, E. W., · · · · · 13 Dunbar Road
SERANUS, · · · · · Conservatory of Music
SHAW, H. N., · · · · · 15 King Street East
SHERLOCK, J. M., · · · · · 30 Lansdowne Avenue
SHIPE, MISS, · · · · · 216 Robert Street
SLATTER, JNO., · · · · · 555 Sherbourne Street
STRAUSS-YOUNGHEART, MME. · · · · · 143 Euclid Avenue
STUTCHBURY, H., · · · · · 542 Parliament Street
SULLIVAN, MISS FANNIE, · · · · · 248 Jarvis Street
TANDY, RECHAB. · · · · ·
TESSEMAN, C. B., · · · · ·
WALDRON, JNO., · · · · · 263 Carlton Street
WARRINGTON, FRED., · · · · · 214 Carlton Street
WELSMAN, FRANK S., · · · · · 266 Sherbourne Street
WIEHMAYER, THEODORE, · · · · · 53 Grenville Street
WILLIAMS, MISS C. A., · · · · · Rossin House

Information as to terms for tuition of the various teachers can always be obtained by application to the publishers, at their office, 32 King Street West, whence also telephone communication can be had direct with any of the profession.

# Grains from a Golden Sheaf.

*Terse sentences from letters recently received by the Mason & Risch Piano Co.,
Limited, from prominent musicians or musical institutions
regarding Mason & Risch Pianos.*

*From Mme. Drechsler Adamson, the well-known Toronto Teacher of Violin:*
"What a wonderful power of standing in tune and resisting climatic influences."

*From Mme. Albani, the greatest of all Vocalists:*
"As a Canadian I feel proud of Mason & Risch pianos."

*From J. Humfrey Anger, Esq., Professor of Harmony at Toronto Conservatory of Music:*
"The Mason & Risch piano is always an up-to-date instrument."

*From Signor Francesco d'Auria, formerly Teacher of Singing at the Toronto Conservatory of Music:*
"I am most happy to express my warm admiration of the qualities of your
instruments. Mme. d'Auria joins me in the above sentiments."

*From John Bayley, Esq., Bandmaster Queen's Own Rifles, Toronto:*
"Mason and Risch pianos afford the highest satisfaction whenever used."

*From Bishop Strachan School for Young Ladies, Toronto (signed by the Lady Principal):*
"Mason & Risch pianos, of which we use a large number, stand the strain of
constant use in a remarkable manner."

*From Arthur Blakeley, Esq., Organist Sherbourne Street Methodist Church:*
"The attributes of Mason & Risch pianos are all that a musician could desire."

*From Rev. B. C. Borden, Principal of Sackville (N.B.) University, which includes what is probably
the largest Ladies' College in Canada:*
"We have purchased from you at various times over twenty Mason & Risch
pianos. They stand the very hard wear well. Our best testimonial is the number
we have purchased from you."

*From A. T. Cringan, Esq., Musical Director of Toronto Public Schools:*
"Mason & Risch pianos are eminently satisfactory in every way."

*From Guiseppe Dinelli, Esq., Professor of Piano Technique at Toronto Conservatory of Music:*
"Mason & Risch pianos have a fine, sympathetic tone, and the touch is perfect."

53

## GRAINS FROM A GOLDEN SHEAF
### (Continued).

❦

*From E. R. Doward, Esq., Organist of the Broadway Tabernacle, Toronto:*

"Mason & Risch pianos are the equal of any made on the continent, and I know of no piano that needs so little tuning."

*From W. E. Fairclough, Esq., Organist of All Saints' Church, Toronto; Musical Director Hamilton Ladies' College, and Professor of Harmony and Pianoforte at Toronto Conservatory of Music:*

"I have always admired the Mason & Risch piano."

*From Edward Fisher, Esq., Director Toronto Conservatory of Music:*

"Mason & Risch pianos are conspicuous for their satisfactory qualities of tone and touch, and at the same time are distinguished for great elegance of design."

*From W. O. Forsyth, Esq., Principal Metropolitan School of Music, Toronto:*

"Mason & Risch pianos possess an individuality of their own."

*From Dr. Albert Ham, Organist St. James' Cathedral, Toronto:*

"I think that your pianos do you infinite credit. The touch and quality of tone are beautifully even throughout."

*From J. W. F. Harrison, Esq., Specialist for Advanced Piano Playing at the Toronto Conservatory; Musical Director Ontario Ladies' College, Whitby; Organist of St. Simon's Church, Toronto:*

"They (Mason & Risch pianos) are artists' instruments. They are particularly admirable from the remarkable manner in which they stand in tune and resist the assaults of hard usage under the most unfavorable conditions."

*From Paul Henneberg, Esq., ex-Principal of Winnipeg Conservatory of Music:*

"Whilst I was connected with the Winnipeg Conservatory of Music it was entirely equipped with Mason & Risch pianos. They were artists' instruments. The wear of any college is great, but to add to this the effects of a Manitoba winter is to put any instrument to a great test. The Mason & Risch pianos stood it, however, and remained an astonishingly long time in tune and wore well."

*From Miss Nora Hillary, Singing Instructress in the Toronto College of Music and many other famous institutions:*

"Of the firm of Mason & Risch I cannot speak too highly. Their pianos have been in use in nearly all the institutions with which I have been connected for nearly twenty years."

*From T. C. Jeffers, Esq., Professor of Advanced Piano Playing and Lecturer of the Toronto College of Music:*

"When played upon a Mason & Risch piano, the finest compositions take on a newer and clearer meaning."

54

## GRAINS FROM A GOLDEN SHEAF

*(Continued).*

✱

*From H. Klingenfeld, Esq., Professor of Violin at Toronto College of Music:*

"The Mason & Risch piano is of the best. Its workmanship is splendid."

*From Miss Ellen M. Knox, Principal of Havergal Ladies' College, Jarvis Street, Toronto:*

"I have found your pianos satisfactory in every respect. Knowing the extreme care taken in their manufacture, I am not surprised to find them so excellent."

*From Durward Lely, the great Scottish Vocalist:*

"Mason & Risch pianos take their place with such instruments as Decker, Weber and Steinway."

*From R. Watkin-Mills, Esq., England's greatest Baritone:*

"Mason & Risch pianos are in every respect first-class instruments."

*From Moulton Ladies' College (signed by the Musical Directress):*

"We have used Mason & Risch pianos here for several years and have found them in every way satisfactory."

*From Mrs. Neville, of Rolleston House Ladies' Seminary:*

"Have used your pianos for years. They have at all times given the utmost satisfaction."

*From Miss B. J. Peters, the most prominent Lady Teacher of Piano Playing in Vancouver, B.C.:*

"The climate of British Columbia is ruinous to most pianos. Mason & Risch pianos have been used here by me and show no signs of depreciation."

*From Miss Norma Reynolds, Professor of Vocal Culture at Toronto Conservatory of Music:*

"The tone of Mason & Risch pianos is particularly adapted for supporting the voice and they keep well in tune, which is certainly something to consider in this climate."

*From Walter H. Robinson, Esq., Professor of Singing at Toronto Conservatory of Music:*

"I am always delighted to have my voice accompanied by a Mason & Risch piano."

*From E. W. Schuch, Esq., a famous Vocal Instructor, formerly Choirmaster St. James' Cathedral, Toronto:*

"My acquaintance with the Mason & Risch piano is of twenty years' standing. I know of no other piano that retains its tone or stands in tune so long."

*From Miss M. B. Sharp, Principal of the Conservatory of Music, Victoria, B.C.:*

"In my opinion, Mason & Risch pianos surpass all others made in Canada and are fully equal to best American makes."

## GRAINS FROM A GOLDEN SHEAF

*(Continued).*

*From Mme. Adele Strauss-Youngheart:*

"I have been much struck with their beauty of tone and their marvellous power of standing in tune."

*From Rechab Tandy, Esq., Vocal Teacher at the Toronto Conservatory of Music:*

"Mason & Risch pianos possess the rare quality of admirably supporting the voice."

*From Joseph Tees, Esq., Choirmaster Grace Church, Winnipeg:*

"Whenever asked advice I recommend a Mason & Risch piano. Your prices not being quite as low as others, my advice is sometimes thrown away. I propose to keep it up, however."

*From the Countess de Tersmeden, famous Swedish Pianist, now resident in Winnipeg:*

"I have used Mason & Risch pianos at my concerts and beg to testify to their beauty of tone and crispness of touch."

*From C. B. Teeseman, Esq., Professor of Singing at the Toronto College of Music:*

"I use a Mason & Risch piano at my home and find it in every respect charming."

*From Miss Veals, of Glen Mawr Ladies' Seminary:*

"I have used many of your pianos for years. There is no question of their musical excellence or durability."

*From A. S. Vogt, Esq., Organist of Jarvis Street Baptist Church:*

"I can speak with confidence of the superior merits of Mason & Risch pianos. The workmanship generally is such as to merit none but the highest praise."

*From Frederick Warrington, Esq., Toronto's favorite Baritone:*

"I always experience pleasure when using Mason & Risch pianos as an accompaniment to the voice."

---

These testimonials all refer to the Mason & Risch piano of to-day. With four or five exceptions, they were all received by us within the last few weeks. Please note how many of the writers refer to over "twenty years' experience" of Mason & Risch pianos. Please observe also that every writer is a person of note whose name is known to thousands and whose opinion is valuable. They are all voluntary tributes. Together they form a wonderful testimony to the extraordinary way in which Mason & Risch pianos stand in tune and resist the severest treatment.

NOTE—The whole of the beautiful cuts which embellish this Souvenir are the work of the Toronto Engraving Co., while the letterpress work was executed by the Miln-Bingham Co., Toronto.